# GOD *in*
# *My* LIFE

*By*

## DONNA K KIRBY

# TABLE OF CONTENTS

# PREFACE

In my sophomore year in junior college, my English professor told me that someday, I would write a book. So now, more than 60 years later, her prediction is finally coming true.

Thanks to my Christian parents, I have been very blessed to have God in my life from a very early age. Over the past 30 or so years, I have been writing down some of my experiences with God in my life. Now, I am putting them together in a book.

I hope you will find them helpful as you continue or begin your walk with God.

# DAY 1:
# BEGINNING

My first memory of my church is that of sleeping on a pew with my family at the age of two. I graduated from that to a Sunday School class and eventually to teaching a Sunday School class. This church supported me through all those days, through my college and seminary days, my teaching days in Ohio, and throughout my 36 years as a missionary in Hong Kong. Now, I'm back in that church again, teaching Sunday School and serving in the ESL ministry.

When I was ten years old, in a special meeting in my church, I invited Jesus into my heart and became a Christ follower. Many in that church helped me grow up in my faith and eventually hear God's call to missions work outside my own country. I was working on the staff at Ridgecrest Baptist Assembly when I heard a missionary speak about the need for people around the world to hear about Jesus. She told the story of ten men carrying a big log, with one man on one end and nine on the other end. She explained that the one man was trying to carry the Good News of Jesus to the entire world while the other nine were telling the Good News to people in the USA. Through this, I felt God's call to go to the world to share the Good News.

God continued to lead me through my college and seminary study, and as I taught high school English and speech and worked in a new church start in northwest Ohio. From there, he led me through an appointment with the International Mission Board of the SBC and through 36 years of teaching high-school English and developing and planting churches in Hong Kong.

It has truly been a wonderful adventure of experiencing God at work in my life. My hope for you is that you can experience this wonderful life. He is there just waiting—invite Him in.

# DAY 2:
# HEAVEN 1

As I stood in the backyard looking up into the blue sky filled with fluffy white clouds, I wondered if my little brother was walking on streets paved with gold or was up there sitting on a cloud playing the harp. I thought the streets paved with gold would be very hot or cold on his bare feet, so I didn't think he would be very happy because he had been active and fun-loving. At age 10, that was my understanding of heaven.

My parents were in the living room with some people from the church. My brother, Tolleson, a year younger than me, had been born with a heart defect. He was not supposed to run or get excited, but he had run to catch the school bus a few days earlier and had collapsed on the bus and never regained consciousness. Someone came to my classroom and took me and my good friend, Myra, to her home. I knew something had happened but did not know what. My friend's mother, a beautician, cut and styled my hair. Later, my parents came for me, and I learned that Tolleson had died.

Tolleson and I were very close; we did all our chores together. We played 'house' by drawing out the rooms in the dirt of our front yard and filling them with stones for different things in the house. We made clothes out of big cottonwood tree leaves using tiny sticks for pins. So I was feeling a great loss without him and wondered about where he was.

Many years later, I read an article in one of the news magazines that talked about heaven. My response was that the article had left out so many things. It is true that we don't know everything about heaven, but the Bible does give us a lot of information about it. So, I determined that I would write a better article about heaven. So, here in the following pages is what I have learned:

# DAY 3:
# HEAVEN 2

Perhaps one of the first things I wondered about heaven was if we would recognize our family and friends when we got there.

When Jesus was raised from the dead, his followers recognized him, but his body was different. He was not limited by time and space; he suddenly appeared, entering a room with locked doors and windows in Jerusalem. He ate some fish that they gave him. Then he disappeared and met them at other times in other places. He walked and talked with 2 people on the road from Jerusalem to Emmaus. At first, they did not recognize him, but when he ate with them, they recognized him, but he immediately disappeared. This activity continued over a period of 40 days before his followers watched him as he was taken up into heaven.

When the early followers asked Paul what kind of bodies they would have after being raised from the dead, he gave an illustration of a seed being planted in the ground and coming up as something entirely different. The human body will return to dust, but it will be raised with a God-like body that is ready for heaven; it will never die. It will be like the body of Christ. (1 Corinthians 15:35-53)

Jesus talked about relationships in heaven. Some religious leaders came to ask him a question, hoping to trap him. They made up a hypothetical situation based on their understanding of their law. Their law said that if a man died without having children, the man's brother was supposed to take his wife and have children for him. In their hypothetical situation, seven brothers followed this law, and when the seventh died, the woman died, too, without children. So they asked Jesus whose wife the woman would be in heaven.

Jesus told them that they did not know the Scriptures or the power of God. Then he said that in the next life, the dead would not marry or be given in marriage but would be like the angels in heaven. (Mark 12:18-27)

So, in heaven, we will know each other, but our bodies and relationships will be different.

# DAY 4:
# HEAVEN 3

Two more questions I had about heaven were: *'Where is it? What is it like?'* For the first one, heaven is where God is. In Solomon's prayer, he asks God to hear his prayer from heaven, his dwelling place. (1 Kings 8:30b). Jesus tells his followers that in His Father's house, there are many rooms and that he will go there and prepare a place for them. (John 14:1-3) When Jesus left them, he was taken up into heaven right before their eyes, and a cloud hid Him from sight. Then, two men dressed in white told them that he had been taken up into heaven and would return at a future time to take them to be with him there. (Acts 1:10-11) He is now at the right hand of God, as Stephen said. (Acts 7:55-56)

In Revelation (21 & 22), John tells of what he saw in his vision about the new heaven and the new earth. God and humans will live together. There will be no more tears, mourning, death, pain, hunger, or thirst. Satan will be cast out, so there will be no more temptation and no more curses. The river of life that is crystal clear will flow from the throne of God down the middle of the great street in the city. There will be trees bearing fruit and the leaves will be for healing. The people will see God, and His name will be on them. There will be no night and no need for the sun or moon as the Lord God will give them light.

The Prophet Isaiah was given some words about the new heaven. He said that the wolf, the lamb, the lion, the cow, and the bear will eat and lie down together and a child will be with them and play near snakes but not be harmed. (Isaiah 11:6-9) Isaiah also foretells that the people will build houses and live in them and that they will plant trees and eat their fruit. They will work and enjoy the work of their hands. (Isaiah 65:22)

From these descriptions, I am reminded of the description of the Garden of Eden, and it makes me think that heaven will be a lot like that. God put Adam and Eve in it and told them to take care of it. They walked and talked with God daily. (Genesis 1 & 2) God said that all he created was good. Perhaps His original plan was for man to live in this 'heaven,' but man chose not to trust God, and thus sin, death, and destruction entered.

# DAY 5:
# HEAVEN 4

I had one more question—Who can go to heaven and how does one get to go there?

In a room in Jerusalem, just before he died on the cross, Jesus told his followers to trust in God and to trust in Him and that he was going to prepare a place for them and would return and take them to be with him. Thomas, one of the 12 followers, told Jesus that they didn't know where he was going and didn't know the way there. Then Jesus told them that he was the way, the truth, and the life. No one would come to the Father except through Him. (John 14:1-6)

The Bible tells us that all humans have done wrong and must be punished. So because of His love for all humans, God took care of this: He sent his son, Jesus, who lived without doing anything wrong, and then he obeyed His Father by dying on the cross to pay for all the sins of humans. A person must trust in God and in Jesus to enter heaven.

Jesus talked about this. He said that people must change and become like little children and urged them to be humble like a child. Becoming childlike is a prerequisite for entering heaven. (Matthew 18:2-3) A child puts faith and trust in people around him who show him love and care. Putting faith and trust in God, who loves and cares for people, is the way to begin experiencing a little of heaven on earth and being ready to go there after death. Have you ever had a feeling of being very close to God through a relationship, an experience, or enjoying the beauty and majesty of the created world? That's a little taste of heaven on earth.

In John's vision in Revelation, he is told about those who will not enter heaven: the 'cowardly, the unbelieving, the vile, the murderers, the sexually immoral, those who practice magic arts, the idolaters and all liars—their place will be in the fiery lake of burning sulfur.' (Revelation 21:8 –NIV)

So the Bible is clear: whoever admits that he has done wrong, asks for forgiveness, truly repents, invites Jesus into his heart and life, and begins making Jesus Lord of his life will begin to experience a little of heaven on earth and then go to be with God forever in heaven in the life after death.

# DAY 6:

# MY DREAM

When I was about 13 years old, I wanted to be a basketball star like my mother, who was one in high school. She was short but very fast and good, so good that someone always took her to and from the games. I have a photo of her and her team members, each dressed in a bloomer-style uniform that covered every part of the body except for the arms.

So, in the 8th grade, I went out for the school team. We practiced during our PE class but needed to stay after school for more practice. I rode the bus to and from school. My family had one vehicle, and we lived about 5 miles out of town on a farm. There was always lots of work to be done, even by us children. No one could come to get me after basketball practice ended, and no one could take me to town for the games in the evening or to get on the bus for the out-of-town games.

I practiced and played hard during PE class. My family finally took me to play at one home game. For most of the game, I sat on the bench, not even having a proper uniform. Our team was far ahead, so the coach finally sent me in for a few minutes. I was very short, and all the players from the other team stood over me while I had the ball, but I quickly threw it through their legs to my teammates. That was my one and only time to play, but I received the praise of my coach and teammates for my quick thinking and handling of the ball.

However, I learned something about my family's priorities. My parent always took us four children to every church activity for our age group or made appropriate arrangements for us to take part in those activities. I learned that teaching us about God and helping us learn to live out our faith in daily life was more important. I now realize that if they had taken me to all those ball games, my life would have been very different.

So, in the ninth grade, I changed from playing basketball to singing in the school chorus, where I got lots of good training in music that has stayed with me throughout my life. I am forever grateful to my parents for this early lesson they taught me by their actions.

# DAY 7:
# GROWING UP IN
# A CHRISTIAN HOME

Proverbs 22:6

Growing up in a Christian home was a real blessing. Our parents always tried to help us in our own Christian growth and experiences by making difficult choices in the things that were important.

Early on, they decided to go into the city to First Baptist Church rather than go to the small country church that was nearby. I came to understand that they made this choice to help us. We took part in many age-related activities and had many Christian friends our age and many Christian adults who taught and helped us.

Mother was the easier-going one, but Daddy was stricter. Whenever we wanted to ask about doing something, we always went to Mother first. But Mother always said, "Go ask your father." They were always on the same page in giving us direction and guidance.

I remember my father as the strict one; one memory stands out. One day, my father told me and my younger brother to stand in one place to make the cows go back into the pasture. Then, he went to find the cows. We waited and waited and soon became tired of waiting and went off to play. Sometime later, after he finally got the cows back in the pasture, he came to find us where we were playing happily.

He very sternly said to us, "When I tell you to do something, you stay and do it no matter how long it takes." Then, he got a switch and gave us both a good switching. That's the only time I remember that my father gave us physical punishment.

I am forever grateful for my Christian upbringing and cannot imagine how different my life would have been without it.

## DAY 8:

# THE BOUNDARY LINES 1

When I was born, the doctor told my father to take care of his wife because the little girl would not live. Well, he was wrong! I have had more than 80 years, and I can say, 'The boundary lines have fallen for me in pleasant places' (Psalm 16:6, NIV).

I was born into a Christian family that taught the Word, lived it out in daily life, and took me to church, where I had a loving, supportive church family for all of my growing up years and into my years of ministry. It was there that I accepted Jesus as my savior and also experienced my beginning call to a life committed to God. Then, I spent 2 years in a small Christian junior college that added to that firm foundation with the support and encouragement of many classmates and teachers. A summer spent on the staff of a Christian retreat center added to that foundation and led to my commitment to serving the Lord outside of my own culture if he continued to lead me in that direction.

Finishing college at a state university with the support of my family broadened my boundary lines beyond my more protected Christian environment and strengthened as well as challenged my faith. Studying for a seminary degree opened up a whole new world as I learned from men and women of God who opened God's word for me to a new depth of meaning. The relationships with fellow students and teachers challenged and broadened those boundary lines mentally, emotionally, and spiritually.

After completing my first year of seminary, a summer spent in New Orleans working in a home for unwed mothers taught me more and challenged me to depend on Him even more. After completing my final year of seminary, I spent the summer in northwest Ohio working in survey and VBS ministry; this moved my boundary lines even further, broadening my experience and helping me learn more about trusting God for daily living and in serving him. This led to my moving to the area to teach school and work in a newly begun church in that area.

# DAY 9:

# THE BOUNDARY LINES 2

A challenging year of teaching that almost made me give up that profession in the end led to a love of teaching that has continued throughout my life. This three-year experience of teaching in high school and working in a new church started in an area not so influenced by Christianity as that of my southern upbringing challenged me and led to my decision to seek God's plan for mission service outside of my own country.

Serving as a missionary in Hong Kong for 36 years was not always easy; it was challenging but also very rewarding. Learning the Chinese language was challenging and a life-long struggle, as was learning to live as an acceptable outsider in another culture. Reading the Bible in another language and seeing that the truths were the same with different words was affirming. Seeing God change individuals through another language and culture affirmed the truth of his word, of his love for all people, and of his plan that all should come to know him. Having the opportunity to teach English in a Chinese high school and work with the Christian program gave me the opportunity to influence many young people who are now serving in many churches around the world. Working with new believers to help them grow in their faith and become leaders in the church was another very rewarding phase. I was truly blessed to have a part in all of this.

And the icing on the cake was an opportunity after retirement to work in mainland China with a service organization using my teaching skills and past experience to help teachers of English improve their own English and teaching methods. Living out my Christian faith without being able to talk about it openly was challenging, but it also taught me a lot about relying on and waiting on the Holy Spirit to work through me and in the lives of others.

Truly, 'the boundary lines have fallen for me in pleasant places' and 'I have a delightful inheritance.' (Psalm 16:6, NIV) A missionary friend shared this verse as he talked about his life. It stuck in my mind, and so I applied it to my life.

# DAY 10:
## GOING TO HONG KONG

Psalm 139:9-10

After saying goodbye to my family at the Atlanta, Georgia airport, feeling both sad and excited, I boarded the plane bound for Hong Kong. After many hours, I landed in Honolulu, Hawaii. I got off and walked around the airport and then boarded the plan again for Tokyo, Japan.

After landing in Tokyo, I deplaned and looked around for someone who was supposed to meet me, but seeing no one, I collected my bags. The airport was extremely crowded; there was a famous person passing through the airport. A redcap offered to take my bags so that I could get a taxi to the hotel where I was to spend the night. He took my bags and hurried off, disappearing into the crowd. I wandered around the airport for a time, thinking and praying about what I should do. Finally, I decided to go to the Japan Airlines desk and tell them what had happened.

When I arrived at the desk and told them what had happened, they brought my bags to me. The red cap had not tried to lose me, but the airport was so very crowded, and to him, I looked no different from many other white foreigners in the airport. I sighed with relief and said a silent prayer of thanks.

I got safely to my hotel and then, the next morning, returned to the airport for the final leg of my journey to Hong Kong. After an uneventful flight, the plane landed in Hong Kong at Kai Tak International Airport. As I deplaned in the open air in front of the airport, I looked up at the top of the building and saw a large crowd of missionaries waving to me. I was so grateful and said a silent prayer of thanks to God for bringing me safely.

After I went through immigration and customs, the group met me and welcomed me warmly. They took my bags, and one drove me to 169 Boundary Street, where I lived for my first two years in Hong Kong. I immediately began studying the Cantonese language with three tutors at home, three hours every afternoon for five days a week, plus using as much time or more to prepare for class. I was too late to enter Language School but decided I would join the class the next semester.

## DAY 11:
# FIRST DAY IN HONG KONG

After a good night's rest in the flat (apartment) I shared with another missionary, the missionary drove us to the outer edge of the city, driving, of course, on the left-hand side of the road as required in a British colony. There was a lot of traffic, but we finally got out of the traffic and came to a quieter place. As we arrived on the top of a hill and looked down below, I saw the bright blue sky with white fluffy clouds above the deep blue ocean. I thought to myself, *Wow! What beauty!*

Then we went down nearer the ocean to an apartment building where six missionary families lived. We parked and entered the apartment of another single missionary friend. After greeting everyone, we sat down at a table set with American utensils and a delicious meal of fried chicken, biscuits, gravy, green beans, and fruit.

I thought to myself, *Wow! Here I am, halfway around the world, and I'm eating as if I were back in Georgia.*

I had many opportunities to eat American food in the homes of different missionary families. In my first home that I shared with an older missionary, we had a Chinese lady who cooked for us. She cooked American food and Chinese food when we asked her to. My housemate and I took turns planning the meals and telling our Chinese helper what to cook. So I had to very quickly learn to speak Cantonese to speak to the helper because she did not understand a lot of English.

Thus began this life of living in a mixture of worlds—American, English, Chinese, and international. As I learned more of the Chinese language (the Cantonese dialect), I began to move more into the Chinese world at church and at the school where I taught.

# DAY 12:
# EATING CHINESE FOOD

I learned to enjoy Chinese food and eventually came to love it, and I became very adept at eating with chopsticks. At almost every Chinese meal, there was something new.

The first time I went to a wedding dinner, the first dish that came out was a bowl of clear broth soup with big black mushrooms and chicken feet sticking out. I ate the soup, and it tasted good. I didn't know quite how to eat the chicken feet but later learned and came to find them quite tasty because of the delicious sauce. I decided that I would continue to try everything.

One challenging experience was when I saw a dish that I thought looked like blood pudding and said to myself, *I don't think I can eat that.*

Sure enough, my friend served me a spoonful as she said, "Have some pig blood pudding."

I managed to eat it but decided that in the future, I would politely refuse.

When the teachers in the school where I taught asked me if I wanted to go eat snake with them, I was hesitant. I could picture taking my chopsticks and picking up a bite of the snake. I was not sure I could do that.

But I went with them and sat at the table with those who did not want to eat snake. Halfway through the meal, my good friend brought me a bowl of soup and asked me to try it. I did, and it was delicious—snake soup.

Most formal meals began with a dish of cold cuts, followed by different dishes of meat, vegetables, seafood, and one or two different soups. It usually ended with fried rice or fried noodles; you could choose one or even try both.

I continued to try everything at least once, and almost everything really tasted good, even the dish of black eel that was a little crunchy.

# DAY 13:

# LEARNING ANOTHER LANGUAGE

Learning a language other than your own native language is challenging. In high school, I took Latin. It was not a spoken language but it was useful for knowing the meaning of a lot of English words. In college, I took Spanish to meet my language requirement. I did well, but the goal was not to speak the language in daily life. Then, in seminary, I took Greek to help me understand the Bible better, but it was not a spoken language.

After I arrived in Hong Kong, I began an intense study of Cantonese, the Chinese dialect spoken there. Being a tonal language made it difficult, and the writing with no alphabet was even more challenging. After some months of study, I decided to go to the local street markets to buy some cloth to make a bedspread. Having learned in language class that the Chinese and English ways of measuring feet and yards were different, I wrote down how much cloth I needed in Chinese measurements and English measurements.

In the market, I found the cloth I liked, and using Cantonese, I bought and paid for the cloth. After arriving home, I proudly showed my housemate what I had been able to do on my own. As she pulled the cloth out of the bag, I realized I had enough for 3 spreads; I had mixed up my English and Chinese numbers. I made a spread for myself, one for my housemate, and one for the couple who lived upstairs!

After about 3 years of intense study of Cantonese, I began teaching English as a second language in a Chinese high school. After another year or so, I begin teaching the Bible in Cantonese to the 12th graders. Before my first class, I had my language helper teach me how to say what I wanted to say to the students. So, in the first class, in my best Cantonese, I said to them, "If you turn in your papers late, I will take off points from your grade."

Some of the boys snickered.

I asked one male student that I knew from church to tell me what I had said. He said, "It's nothing. It is ok."

So, after class, I went downstairs and said it to one of the English teachers. She laughed and told me I had said I would propose marriage if they handed in their papers late. Just a small difference in the tone of one word made a big difference!

# DAY 14:

# EXPERIENCING GOD'S LOVING CARE, 1

Isaiah 26:3-4

As I left school to walk home, a fellow teacher took my letters to mail them for me, and I then walked straight home and entered my apartment building through the back door. When I came to the back door of my apartment, I saw the door knob hanging down, and the door was slightly ajar. Someone had broken in.

I quickly went to the front of the building and got the watchman. As we stood there looking at my back door and talking, suddenly a young man appeared. He saw us and quickly turned and ran out the front door. We ran back to the front gate at the bottom of the stairs. He saw us standing there and quickly turned and ran up 10 floors of stairs, across the rooftop, and down the back stairs. We called the police, and the watchman went to the back door and caught the young man with the bag of items that he had taken from the apartment. He was a recent immigrant from China.

The policemen arrived quickly, took the young man, and then looked carefully through my apartment. As they searched the apartment, I sat and talked with one of the policemen. I learned that he had been to church with some of his friends, the same church that I went to. Before I left for the USA, I asked a young man from my Bible class to follow up with him.

Before the policeman left, they asked me to make a list of all the missing items and bring it to the police station. The police took the bag of items to hold as evidence until the time of the trial.

I had a Chinese friend staying with me as she waited for her visa to immigrate to Canada. She came home later after the police had left. I told her what had happened, and we made a list of the things missing from her room and from my room. That night, as I looked around my room, I found a knife under the chair at my desk. The police had missed it. I also found a note on my desk written by the thief: *'Sorry, Missy.'*

## DAY 15:

# EXPERIENCING GOD'S LOVING CARE, 2

The next day, we took the knife, the note the thief had left for me, and our lists of missing items to the police station. We were told it would probably be about a month before we could get our things back. We told them that my friend was leaving for Canada soon, and I was leaving for the USA in a few weeks. We hoped we could get everything back before that.

The case was finished, and we got all our items back before my friend left and before I left for the USA. However, one of my diamond rings was missing. There was no explanation.

Through all of this, I was grateful for God's loving care and the quiet peace that he gave. If I had mailed my letters as I had intended, I would have walked home a different way and entered the front door, walking in on the burglar possibly with his knife in hand. With the help of the watchman, the burglar was caught, and the watchman was unharmed because the burglar had left his knife inside. The police handled the case effectively so that we got back the stolen items in good time. My Chinese friend had not walked in on the burglar because she had come home later.

Several months later, after returning from my stateside leave, I was cleaning out the room that my friend had stayed in. Under the bed, I found an old airline bag with a slit in the bottom. I had never seen it before and wondered where it had come from. I examined it, and as I did, the missing diamond ring fell out! The bag had belonged to the burglar. He had taken my friend's new bag and slit the old bag to let the stolen items fall into the new bag and then pitched the old one bag under the bed. Mystery of the missing ring solved!

## DAY 16:

# THE GOSPEL FOR ALL PEOPLE AND CULTURES

I had the privilege of seeing God at work in another language and culture. This strengthened my faith and my conviction that the Gospel is true and is for all people in all languages and cultures.

I met a lady and her son living in a government low-cost housing project. She was handicapped and used a wheelchair. She and her son lived in a small one-room apartment with a part walled off for a bedroom and a tiny kitchen. The bathroom was on the balcony. The apartment was one of many hundreds in that building, which was surrounded by many more such buildings.

I visited several times, and they soon became Christ's followers. As you entered the apartment, you would look straight ahead at a wall that had an altar for worshiping idols and ancestors. After they became believers, the mother wanted to know what she should do with that altar. She agreed that they should get rid of it and asked for the help of a local pastor and me to take it down. One day, we went and helped her take it down and put it in the trash. The wall looked so very empty to her, so she asked what she could put up in place of the altar. We suggested that she put some flowers there to remind her of God, who created everything and created beautiful flowers for us to enjoy. She did do that.

This reminded me of Jesus' words in Luke 11:24-26. The demon or evil spirit was driven out of the man, and his heart swept clean. The demon returned because nothing was put in to replace what had been driven out. This points to the importance of helping new believers fill their hearts and minds with God's word. In addition to filling that wall, this woman and her son continued to fill their hearts and lives with learning more and following after God and worshiping Him.

# DAY 17:
## WHAT'S IN A NAME?

When I was born, I was named Donna Kay Kirby. Growing up, I was called Donna, but because I was short, I was sometimes called 'Shortie.' When I became a teacher, I was called Miss Kirby. When I arrived in Hong Kong as a missionary with the IMB, my language teacher gave me the name Gwoo *Dung Laan*, the surname coming first, followed by the first and second name. The meaning of the name is 'Caring for winter orchids.' So in language school, I was *Gwoo Siu Je,* my Chinese surname and title for a young lady.

As I took part in a Chinese church, some called me Miss Kirby or *Gwoo Shoon Gau See*, the title for a missionary, and a few close friends called me Donna. When I began teaching in a Chinese High School, in English class, I was Miss Kirby, or if the students forgot to say the 'Miss' first, I sometimes was Kirby Missy. Some would address me in Chinese as *Gwoo Seen Saang*, my surname, followed by the title of 'teacher.'

When I began working full time in a small Chinese Baptist Church, I was most often called *Gwoo Gwoo*

*Neurng,* my surname followed by the title for a single woman church worker. Needless to say, I learned to answer to all of these names, and the name helped me to identify where I knew the person and helped me to recall the name of the person.

One evening, I was in a busy, crowded restaurant in Wan Chai, Hong Kong, when I heard someone call out, "Miss Kirby."

I turned and looked and saw this young man dressed in a sailor's uniform. I did not recognize him but was intrigued and went over to talk to him. He told me who he was and that I had taught him in a high school in northwest Ohio several years earlier. I had about 90 different students for each of the 3 years I taught there and was pleased that he remembered me even though I didn't remember him.

So, what's in a name? A name can bring back a lot of memories of past experiences and relationships. Being called 'Christian' brings up the most important relationship of all. The Bible says the followers of Jesus were first called 'Christians' at Antioch as a somewhat derogatory title. (Acts 11:26b). May our lives bring honor to that 'Name Above All Names.'

## DAY 18:

# CELEBRATING CHRISTMAS IN HONG KONG

My first Christmas in Hong Kong was different. It was very warm, and there were 4-foot-tall poinsettias growing in many places outside.

I celebrated in my Chinese church on Christmas Eve with a big Chinese dinner and program. The children acted out the Christmas story, with little children in 'sheep clothing' crawling around on the stage. On Christmas Day, I went to the Christmas worship service.

I returned home, and my housemate and I packed a picnic lunch and drove out to the New Territories. We stopped at a beautiful park and ate our lunch surrounded by very tall poinsettias. Then, we went on to visit some of my housemate's friends, three Chinese teenage girls that she was caring for; this care was passed to her by an older missionary friend.

For the following Christmases, I tried to combine my Chinese celebrations with my American traditional celebrations with some of my single missionaries. I decorated a live Christmas tree in my home and had some of the students from the school where I taught to come for a party. On Christmas Eve, I went to the Christmas celebration at my church and then to the worship service on Christmas morning. Afterward, I dashed across the harbor to a missionary friend's home, where we all contributed to a traditional Christmas lunch and gift sharing.

One Christmas stands out in my memory. I went to the Christmas Eve service at my Chinese church and then to the Christmas Day worship service. Since my missionary friends were away from Hong Kong, I did not have any plans for joining them. After the worship service, I hoped I would be able to join some of my Chinese church friends to celebrate with them, but no one invited me; they all had their plans and disappeared.

So, feeling very sorry for myself, I took the bus downtown and ate a lonely Christmas dinner at the Hilton Hotel Coffee shop. I continued with the not-very-tasty dinner, still feeling sad, alone, and sorry for myself. BUT I made a decision—I would prevent this from ever happening again. For future Christmases, I would not wait on invitations from others but would take the initiative to plan and invite others for a Christmas celebration.

# DAY 19:

# LANGUAGE SCHOOL

When the new semester began at the language school, I joined the beginning class. In my class, there were a couple from another Christian mission group, a Catholic priest, and another guy from another Christian mission group. My tutors had prepared me well; I fit right in with the class. The Catholic priest was very good, but the rest of us were about the same in ability. We had three hours in class with a different teacher each hour. I continued to study this way for two years. At the end, we had a graduation ceremony; one person from our class was to make a speech. We unanimously sent the Catholic priest because he was so good. After graduation, we all went our separate ways to various ministries.

One of our teachers, Mr. Jek, always made fun of my name; I never learned why. It had been given to me by Mr. Ho, one of the teachers who worked with most of us from our mission. He wanted to make the Chinese name sound like our English name but also have a good meaning. Mine meant caring for winter orchids, and the given name sounded very much like my English name. I liked it very much, even though it was difficult to write—the surname had twelve strokes, and the second name had fifteen strokes. The first name had only three strokes, so every time I signed my name, I had to make thirty marks in the proper way.

Every day, we had a break time; we all went to the canteen and practiced our language skills to order snacks and drinks. One day, I wanted to buy a small Coke. The person handed me this very large Coke. I had the sounds right but I had used a low tone instead of a mid-level tone. From that experience, I learned how important it was to get the tones right.

Learning the language was a life-long challenge. I continued studying with tutors for all of my years there. I concentrated on the spoken language but did not continue with writing. I concentrated on reading the writing and being able to turn it into the spoken language because the way it is spoken is not the way it is written.

## DAY 20:
# TASTE AND SEE

Psalm 34:8; 1 Peter 2:3

The first time I ate the Asian fruit called durian, I ate it at the home of my Chinese friends. After dinner, my host brought a plate of fruit into the living room and asked me to try it. I ate one piece; it had the soft, smooth texture of an avocado and a very light, sweet, addicting flavor (a cross between a peach and a mango) that I had never tasted before. I immediately liked it.

Later, when I saw the fruit in the market and smelled it, I was surprised. It had a very prickly outer covering that hurt your hand when you touched it and a very strong bad smell—somewhat like cat urine and rotten eggs. One time I was in Singapore and bought one to take home to eat. As soon as we got into a taxi, the driver asked, 'Who has some durian?' I said I did, and he immediately got out and put it in the trunk of the taxi until we arrived home. So I learned that some people like durian very much, but some can't stand it.

Once, when I was in the USA on a home assignment and taking part in a mission conference, a person who was interviewing several missionaries asked us to talk about something in our adopted culture that tasted very bad. One man talked about durian saying that it smelled so bad that he just could not eat it. I immediately said that I loved the soft, rich, smooth taste, even though it smelled bad. This experience emphasized once again two different reactions to the same thing.

Many times, people's response to Jesus and the Christian faith is like that—some people have never tasted or even tasted but still are strongly opposed. Others have tasted and know the joys even when they encounter difficulties after tasting.

What about you? Will you taste and see that the Lord is good? Have you already tasted that the Lord is good? Will you keep on tasting and growing up in him?

## DAY 21:

# WHEN WE DON'T HAVE THE WORDS TO PRAY

Romans 8:26-27 (NIV)

For me, prayer is the foundation for my relationship with God and the source of wisdom and strength for daily living. So, I wanted to learn to pray in my adopted language—Cantonese. But I found it difficult. Like us, when we pray before others, Chinese Christians also use special language.

My language teacher helped me learn the phrases for the beginning—addressing God and thanking him, and then the ending phrases.

He said to me, "What's in the middle is up to you."

So, one day at our meeting after school for a group of about 40 girls—we called it GAs—we were dedicating the new leaders for the year. The teacher I worked with called on me to pray for the new leaders. In those few seconds, I thought, *These girls don't understand English. I need to pray in Cantonese.*

So, I opened my mouth with the beginning phrases I had learned, and I remembered using the closing words, but I didn't remember anything in between.

After the meeting, the teacher said to me, "Donna, I didn't know you could pray so well in Cantonese."

I said, "Oh, really!?"

As I walked home from school with my housemate, a short-term missionary journeyman, I told her about it.

She said, "When I heard you begin in Cantonese, I prayed for you."

When I didn't know what to pray, the Holy Spirit helped me. I wish I could say that, after that, it was very easy, but it took a lot more practice. However, praying in the local language led to deeper fellowship with local believers, and I learned that God hears prayers from the heart, even if they are filled with language errors.

# DAY 22:
# MISUSED AND CRITICIZED

As a missionary teacher working in a Hong Kong high school, I went into the principal's office to chat with her about a situation in which I needed her help. Some of the homeroom teachers were not sitting with their classes during the chapel service. Sometimes, the program that I helped plan and carry out needed the teachers to help their class take part in the appropriate way, but they were not present. I wanted her to encourage them to sit with their class as they were supposed to do. Perhaps I had a little bit of an ulterior motive—wanting all teachers to obey the rules.

Before the next time, we had a chapel service. She went to each of the three rooms for teachers and required all of them to go to the chapel service, even those who were not homeroom teachers.

At the next teachers' meeting, she very sweetly thanked me for telling her that some teachers were not going to the chapel service. I wanted to reply, but she did not give me a chance, and I didn't know what to say or how to respond in Cantonese. She had misused my words to be able to do what she wanted to do and in a back handed way to criticize me before all the teachers. She had done this to other teachers and not let them respond, but she had never done it to me.

After the teachers' meeting, as we teachers walked out, they all gathered around me to sympathize with me and support me. At that moment, I felt that I was really a part of the teaching staff, loved and accepted even though I was a foreigner not paid by the school. I had tried hard to be an acceptable outsider and build good relationships with the teachers so that I could encourage the believers and share the Good News in an acceptable way with the non-believers. This painful experience helped me be much closer to them.

As we live in this world, we must make many difficult decisions. Galatians 5:25 says: 'Since we live by the Spirit, let us keep in step with the Spirit.' (NIV) May it be our desire that all we do, think, feel, and say be in step with the Holy Spirit in us.

# DAY 23:

# RESPONDING TO MISUE AND CRITICISM

After the principal misused my words and criticized me before all the teachers, I wanted to do something to put this behind me and clear up the relationship. I invited the principal to have lunch with me one day so that we could talk and renew the relationship. We had a good talk, and I felt I was okay with the relationship.

In the coming days and weeks before the end of the school year, I began to think more about why I had come to Hong Kong and why I was in that school. I came to feel that 'holy unrest' that made me think it was time to make a change. I needed to leave the school, but I had no idea where I should go—*to another school or to another kind of ministry.* I made the decision to leave without knowing where I would go.

On a Sunday, soon after that, my pastor preached on Abraham and how God called him to go to a place without knowing where he was to go. This affirmed my decision.

As I prayed and talked with others, I was seeking God's clear guidance. When I talked with my pastor, he invited me to come and work with them on the church staff. This was the mother church for the school and the one I had been serving in in various ways for about 20 years. However, I did not feel that was the right place for me.

Then I talked with my very good friend who was the principal of another Baptist school, and she invited me to come and teach there. I prayed and thought about it, and it seemed that this was the right place for me for the time being. This would give me more time to use the skills I already had and explore other areas of ministry. I taught a class of 8th graders and, outside of class, helped some students who had recently come from China and needed remedial help. It was a good year.

By the end of the year, I felt God leading me to be a part of the staff of my church that I had been a part of for 20 years. So I made the move with the support of my mission organization. God led me through having me face a problem and learning it was time to move to a new ministry.

## DAY 24:
# FACING CRITICISM

Psalm 31:24 (NIV)

Sunday afternoon, the phone rang. It was a fellow deaconess at my church. She said the other deaconesses had asked her to call me and tell me that I should change my ways of doing things. When I asked her what she meant, she just said that I knew what I was doing. After insisting that I had no idea what she meant, we hung up.

My first response was to want to find out what they were talking about and fight back against what they were supposing that I had done. As I thought more about it, I was upset because I knew that someone closer to me had spoken to them about me. I was not involved in activities at church with them except for the monthly Deacon's Meeting. Still thinking about the conversation, I thought over all my ministries in the church and still could not think of anything that they might be talking about.

For about two weeks, I continued to be very upset—to the point I was not able to eat or sleep well. I was the missionary who had come across the world and had worked so hard to learn the language and get very involved in ministry in the church and in the school that the church sponsored. I felt I was doing a very good job and that they were being unfairly critical of me.

After two weeks, when I met with my prayer partner, who knew all the deaconesses well, I shared with her and asked her if I should try to talk to them and find out what they meant. She thought it would not be wise to do that and suggested that I think about it this way—they did not want to harm me but felt that they meant it for my good. I had not thought about it in that way. After sharing more and praying together, I was able to let it go.

I did one more thing to help me put it behind me and restore the relationship. At the next meeting, I sat next to the deaconess who had called me and gave her a piece of homemade apple pie, which I knew she loved. I also asked her if she had anything to send to her friend in the States because I was going in a few weeks. In the following times together, I was able to continue in ministry with them without any hard feelings.

# DAY 25:

# KNOWING BLACK AMERICANS

Growing up on a farm in Georgia in the 1940s, the only African Black Americans I knew were the uneducated men who worked for my father and two women named Gertrude and Ceebee. The men worked for a week, and then after my father had paid them, they disappeared until they had used up all their money for gas, drinking, or gambling.

Gertrude and Ceebee loved to sit on the banks of our pond and fish all day. They taught me to fish. I would sit with them until I got bored; then, I would stick my pole in the ground and go off to play. I would come back later to see if, by chance, I had a fish on my pole; they were still sitting there.

My first year at seminary, I met for the first time, an educated black American woman, named Dora. We became good friends over the two years at the seminary and kept in contact after we graduated. She became a missionary for the Home Mission Board, SBC (now the North American Mission Board), and I became a missionary with the Foreign Mission Board,

SBC (now the International Mission Board) and was appointed to Hong Kong.

I came home on furlough (now Stateside Assignment) some years later. I got back in touch with Dora and invited her to come visit me. After she came to visit me, we planned to go to my church on Wednesday night. The thought occurred to me, *Will she be welcomed at my church?* Then I thought, *Maybe it will be ok if I introduce her as a missionary with our board.*

So, we walked into church with me feeling concerned, but everyone welcomed her warmly. I breathed a sigh of relief, but I also realized there would be some time before we all could live in harmony with mutual respect, no matter what our race and position.

Jesus tells us to 'Love your neighbor as yourself.' (Luke 10:27b NIV).

Then, through the story, he tells about the good Samaritan (Luke 10:30-37 NIV) in answer to the question, 'Who is my neighbor?' we know that we are to help anyone who needs help without giving attention to race, color, or creed.

May we all obey Jesus' words: 'Go and do likewise.'

## DAY 26:

# HOLY DISSATISFACTION

For some days, I had been feeling what I call a holy dissatisfaction. I was feeling discouraged by the difficulties arising in several areas of ministry and the lack of people coming forward to help. I was wondering if I should be doing more or make a change in my service to the Lord, even look for another church. I was drawn to several possibilities that seemed to fit my skills and gift—teaching English as a second language in another place, helping in an international ministry in another area, and training ESL volunteer teachers for a nearby mission organization. I continued to pray and asked the Lord what I should do.

In my quiet time one morning, God gave me 2 Chronicles 32:7—'Be strong and courageous. Do not be afraid or discouraged…for there is a greater power with us than with him.' (NIV) These words spoke to my present situation.

A few days later, God gave me these verses, Isaiah 54:1-2, and I claimed them as my verses for the rest of the year. Yes, although single, I had many spiritual children scattered around the US and the world; however, I needed to continue to spread my tent.

Several days later, in the middle of the day, as I was going about my regular routine, a clear thought suddenly entered my mind—stay and go deeper in your present relationships and ministry. I felt this was God's answer to me and an indication of how I was to spread my tent. I began doing just that and continued to ask almost daily, how he wanted me to go deeper with people and ministry. In the days that followed, he began to put individual people on my heart and helped me reach out to them and affirmed me in those efforts. He had begun to raise up the help needed in the ministries I was involved in. As I kept on keeping on he kept on guiding and encouraging me. (Jeremiah 29:11-13)

## DAY 27:

# AFFIRMATION OF GOD'S WILL

At the age of 68, after five years of comfortable retirement life in very easy-going, peaceful surroundings, I decided to return to my previous mission field to work as an English consultant with a local Christian organization. Basing this decision mainly on my good health and that I had the language and cross-cultural skills needed for the task, I felt this was God's leading for me at the time.

After arriving on the field, I settled in rather quickly and immediately helped carry out a week-long English workshop for 60 middle school English teachers. Everyone said that it was the most successful one they had ever had. In the following months, I mainly observed, listened, and learned more about the situation and the needs.

During these months, I wavered back and forth between missing my comfortable retirement life and seeing the needs and opportunities for making a difference in the lives of the local English teachers. I realized I had forgotten about some of the difficulties in living there: huge crowds of people, constant movement and noise, fast pace of life, and pollution. In addition, my travel to the workplace was a tiring and boring 4-hour bus ride, which I made every two to three weeks.

Also within those first six months, I had almost every minor illness from my previous years but which I had not experienced in the last five to six years: swollen, painful right ankle, excess wax in my ear, hemorrhoids, a bad cold, and an ear infection. On the other hand, several things had worked out so smoothly: successfully adjusting to the work culture of the organization and getting my work permit, ID card, and multiple entry visas, making it very easy for me to go in and out of the work area. So, I wavered back and forth in my thinking and praying, asking God if I was in the right place or if I had misunderstood His leading.

One day, I was studying 1 Corinthians 16:5-9, when verse 9 caught my attention. Paul had decided to stay longer in Ephesus even though there were many who opposed him he felt there was a great door for effective work open for him. God affirmed that even though I had faced difficulties, there was an open door for effective work. So I stayed.

# DAY 28:
# EXPERIENCING THE PRESENCE OF GOD 1

Matthew 28:20b

After being retired for five years, I returned to the area where I had lived and worked for 36 years and began working as an English consultant with a local organization. We had planned and carried out a successful week-long English camp in the summer and a reunion of the participants in the fall. Now, we were planning a day-and-a-half workshop for 60 middle school English teachers to be held at Christmas.

On December 20, I finished the preparations and made the 4 ½ hour trip to the area of work. When I arrived that evening, I noticed a rash and some blisters on my left front upper shoulder. I called the president of our organization and asked him to contact our nurse colleague to find out what doctor I could see. She set it up for me to see one, and I went immediately to see him. He thought it had something to do with osteoporosis and gave me some medicine. The next day, I was feeling much more pain, and the rash had spread to my neck and back upper shoulder, so I went to the clinic again and saw a different doctor. She made the correct diagnosis—shingles—and gave me a different medicine.

The workshop began the next morning, December 23, and I felt well enough to finish the morning session, but then I began to be in more pain, so I went home to rest. By evening, I was in great pain, so a local helper accompanied me to a skin specialist. As soon as the doctor saw me, she knew exactly the illness and the great pain I was in. She immediately gave me medicine through an IV drip along with other pills. After taking the medicine, I felt much better and was able to sleep.

The next day, December 24, I turned over my responsibilities for the workshop to others and followed the doctor's advice to take another dose by IV drip. I was supposed to go back to Hong Kong on the bus with the other volunteers at noon, but I had not finished the medication, so I decided to stay. The medicine made me feel better.

## DAY 29:

# EXPERIENCING THE PRESENCE OF GOD 2

1 Peter 5:7

That evening, our staff and some of the volunteers discussed whether I should stay inland or travel back to Hong Kong with some of the volunteers the next day. I really didn't know what to do. Inland, I stayed in our staff quarters where there were people who could help look after me, but in Hong Kong, I lived alone. I would need to rely on my friends to come and help me, but I felt that I might get more effective medical care in Hong Kong and have more freedom in communicating with friends and family there. So that night, we all prayed and said we would make a decision the next morning. As I prayed, I asked God to give me very clear guidance on what I should do and confirm to me that he was with me no matter what.

I went to bed and slept for about 4 hours. Then I woke up and went into the bathroom to put on the lotion that the doctor had given me to relieve the pain and itching. As I walked into the bathroom, I felt God's presence very strongly, as if he were saying to me: *I'm with you, and you need to stay and not leave with the volunteers.*

I went back to bed and slept until morning. It was December 25, Christmas morning. I had planned to be back in Hong Kong and go to my church for the Christmas worship service and dinner in the evening. This was the first Christmas that I had ever been completely alone, without family, and not being able to join Christian brothers and sisters in worship and celebration. But I was reminded that I was not alone— Emmanuel, God was with me!

So, that morning, I had my own Christmas worship by singing some Christmas hymns, reading Scripture, and praying and praising God.

# DAY 30:

# EXPERIENCING THE PRESENCE OF GOD 3

Isaiah 41:10

When the head of our organization came in to see me later on Christmas Day, I told him that God had affirmed to me that I was to stay inland and go to see the doctor there for one more treatment. I did that later in the day and felt well enough after a good night's rest to return to Hong Kong the next day with other staff members who were going.

Back in Hong Kong, I saw our company doctor, and he gave me medication for pain so that I could sleep at night. The pain was so severe that I couldn't endure clothing on the affected area; it was very cold, so I had to keep my little electric heater on high to try to stay warm. Several friends came on different days to bring food and care for me. I did not leave the house for about two weeks except to go to the doctor every three days. The pain did not abate.

In two more weeks, I was supposed to fly to the USA for a one-month leave. The trip would take about 24 hours from my home in Hong Kong to my home in the USA. I didn't think I could endure the pain for that long. I talked to God about this and asked others to pray for me. I began to feel a little bit better. On the day before I was to fly, I awoke feeling much better and even went to the worship service at a church near my home.

After lunch, I still felt so good that I called a friend and met her to do some shopping for things I needed to take to the USA. And we had afternoon tea before I went home. The next day, I traveled home safely, free of pain. Through this, God taught me to trust him and wait patiently for his perfect plan.

# DAY 31:
# GOD'S PLAN

After the lumpectomy to remove a very small cancer, I received good news that the tumor was removed and there was no cancer in the lymph nodes. No radiation and chemo were recommended, but a medicine was recommended to decrease the risk of reoccurrence. I investigated the three recommended medicines, and then when I saw the doctor, he said the medicines would cut the risk of reoccurrence by half. I chose the one that would not require me to take another medicine to prevent bone density loss. When I filled the prescription, the information clearly told of the risk of uterine cancer as one of the side effects. I had read that, but it had not really made an impression on me. I began taking the medicine and experienced some side effects that subsided after a week.

However, as I thought more and read more about the risk of uterine cancer, I wondered if I had made the wrong choice. I was concerned about bone density loss, but I knew bone density loss could be checked by a scan, and then, if needed, I could take another medicine. The more I thought about it, the more concerned I became about putting myself at risk for another cancer in order to reduce the reoccurrence.

In my quiet time, as I followed my plan to read the Bible through, I came to Jeremiah 29:11-13—"For I know the plans I have for you," declares the Lord, "plans to prosper you and not to harm you, plans to give you hope and a future. Then you will call upon me and come and pray to me, and I will listen to you. You will seek me and find me when you seek me with all your heart" (NIV).

God spoke to my heart, reminding me that my future and hope were dependent on God and not on my choice of medicine. So I decided to continue taking it for the coming months as planned; the side effects came back at the beginning of the second month. I continued to monitor the effects as I continued to listen for God's plan. I could re-evaluate at the end of the three months and make another choice.

# DAY 32:
# SNAKES

I know that in the Bible, it says that after God completed his work of creation, he said that it was all good. That, of course, included snakes, but for me, the only good snake is a dead one.

Growing up in an old farmhouse, I remember finding a snake in the hallway and another time when my older sister and brother made me step over a curled-up snake on our walk in the woods.

More recently, my nephew helped me get a snake out of my garage. Also I saw a long black snake several times in the yard and on the driveway where my neighbor and I walked. I named him Oscar to make him seem less intimidating to me.

Even more recently, I found a five-foot-long snake skin in my basement. I called animal control, and a man came and searched the basement, with me following fearfully behind him. He found nothing and said since there was no food and water there, the snake probably just shed his skin and went back out.

A week or two later, the five-foot-long snake skin was there again in exactly the same place. I called animal control again, and a person came and looked but could not find it. He suggested plugging all the holes around the house. When the snake skin appeared again in the same place a few weeks later, he came and plugged up all the holes. As we stood talking, he happened to notice that the clothes dryer was pulled out from the wall, leaving a very big hole; that's where the snake was coming in. We fixed that, and I did not find another skin in the basement.

One day, I came home from church and pulled up before my garage door. I saw a large stick lying in the driveway, so I got out to pick it up rather than drive over it. It was a 5-foot-long black snake! My nephew came, and we tried to get it to go away from the house, but it went right back to the wall where the hole had been, so we left it there.

Rationally, I know that black snakes are not poisonous, are classified as good snakes, and are a part of God's good creation, but that doesn't make me like them.

# DAY 33:
# GETTING OLD

Getting old isn't easy. Taking a shower only takes about three minutes, but all the other stuff takes much longer. For example, putting medicine on the fungal toenail, putting Vaseline between the toes to keep them from rubbing, putting lotion over the whole body of dry, wrinkled skin, putting body powder between the parts that rub together, washing around dry eyes with baby shampoo, and putting in artificial tears, putting moisturizer on the face and cream on the dark circles under the eyes. Then I'm ready for bed.

But getting a good night's sleep isn't easy. It's difficult to fall asleep and stay asleep. After getting up once or twice during the night to go to the bathroom, often going back to sleep takes a while.

And there are other things that I can't do, for example, opening a bottle of water or a jar of food. So, learning to admit this and ask for help is a new stage.

But I am thankful to be alive.

Having Jesus Christ in my life gives meaning and purpose and the encouragement to keep on keeping on as I do all of my stuff, that is do my part to work with God and reach out to others around me. For I know it is God who gives life and God who ends life. I need to do my part to keep in step with Him for life, however long or short. So I choose not to do anything to keep my hair from being grey. I see it as a God-given 'crown of splendor...attained by a righteous life.' (Proverbs 16:31, NIV)

And I look to the advice given by the writer of Ecclesiastes in 8:15: 'So I commend the enjoyment of life, because nothing is better for a man under the sun than to eat and drink and be glad. Then joy will accompany him in his work all the days of the life God has given him under the sun.' (NIV)

## DAY 34:

# EXPERIENCING GOD'S PRESENCE IN FACING DIFFICULTY 1

About a week after my annual mammogram, I received a call to come back for a second look with an ultrasound. After the ultrasound, the doctor said there was a mass that was not on the previous mammogram and that a biopsy needed to be done.

Because I was waiting for another medical report and I was going on a family vacation after a week, I decided to do nothing at the time. In my quiet time one morning, in my daily Bible reading of Exodus, God spoke through Exodus 15:26d—"For I am the Lord Who heals you' (NIV).

My primary care doctor called and suggested I see a breast surgeon for follow-up. The next day, God spoke to me through the daily reading from the devotional book *DAY BY DAY,* p. 196: 'Do not allow difficult events to cancel the joy of knowing you are a child of God. Choose to allow God's Spirit to fill you with His unquenchable joy, and your life will be a miracle to those who watch you face the trials that come.'

After I returned from my vacation with my family, I called and set up an appointment to see the recommended surgeon. She set up an appointment for an ultrasound-guided biopsy two weeks later.

While still waiting, God continued to speak. One morning, as I read Exodus 13:21-22, he affirmed that as he had led his people through the desert, he would lead me on this medical journey.

One Sunday morning during worship, we sang the hymn, *LEANING ON THE EVERLASTING ARMS*. The words reminded me that I only needed to lean on him to be 'safe and secure from all alarms.'

God continued to speak as I read *EXPERIENCING GOD DAY BY DAY,* July 5 and 8; he reminded me that my joy came from the Holy Spirit in me so that my life would be a testimony to others. I asked God to help me on this medical journey to have joy and let others see God in me.

## DAY 35:

# EXPERIENCING GOD'S PRESENCE IN FACING DIFFICULTY 2

I went in for the ultrasound-guided biopsy of a nodule in my right breast. It went smoothly, and as I was waiting for the doctor to tell me I could leave, the tech came in and said the doctor wanted to talk to me. She took me back into the procedure room and had me sit on the examination table. Then the doctor said that the nodule they had biopsied was not the one identified and marked on the original mammogram and on the first ultrasound. She did not say she had made a mistake or biopsied the wrong nodule.

Normally, I would have reacted very strongly to such a situation. I was shocked and stunned and wondered how this could have happened. As I think back, three people were standing there waiting to see what I would do and say. My mind was in turmoil, but the sentence that came out of my mouth to the doctor was, "It's not an exact science, is it?"

This gave her an out, and she agreed with me. Then my mind quickly turned to what to do; I asked her if I needed another biopsy. She said yes and that it would have to be a different kind and a more complicated procedure. Then I asked if it could be done that same day. She told me yes, but that I would have to wait another 30 minutes to set up the equipment.

I waited in the waiting room, and the tech showed me special kindness by bringing me juice and pretzels. The procedure was done well and went smoothly under the very professional head technician.

At the end, the first tech brought me a gift packet and thanked me for being such a good patient. I told her that my Christian faith requires me to behave well even in adverse situations.

I feel that the Holy Spirit guided my response, both in words and actions, by giving me a calm spirit, wisdom, and understanding so that others could see how my faith helped me in my daily actions and choices. (Proverbs 9:10 (NIV); James 3:13-17 (NIV).)

## DAY 36:

# EXPERIENCING GOD'S PRESENCE IN FACING DIFFICULTY 3

While waiting for the biopsy report, God spoke through another devotional book, one that I had read five years earlier but decided to read again—*MY UTMOST FOR HIS HIGHEST.* The verse for August 12—Matthew 8:26, which reads, 'You of little faith, why are you so afraid?' (NIV) went straight to my heart.

When I got the biopsy report, the surgeon said I needed surgery, but the tumor was very small, slow growing, well-behaved, and wouldn't need radiation or chemo, but because it was outside the duct, she would have to check the lymph nodes and remove any with 'hot spots.' This was encouraging, but I still needed wisdom to set up the time for the surgery. It was a very busy time as I was working with people from my church to get ready for the new ESL classes beginning in September. I was enlisting teachers, leading a teachers' meeting, and setting up and carrying out registration. Also I had signed up a year earlier to go to a once in 5-years retreat of fellow retired missionaries. I had planned to teach my ESL class for the first week and then had arranged for a substitute teacher while I went to the retreat for a week. I teach the beginning level; it takes about a month to get them into the learning process and for me to know their level, so it is not good to be away so much in the beginning weeks.

My surgeon said it was all right to wait, so she and her team helped me decide on a time about two months later for the pre-op procedures, surgery, and post-op procedures without affecting my teaching schedule except for one week. This let me get the ESL program up and running, go to the retreat, and have time to get my class stable and find a suitable substitute teacher. This seemed to be God's best timing. I began to feel some peace. (John 14:27—NIV)

# DAY 37:

# EXPERIENCING GOD'S PRESENCE IN FACING DIFFICULTY 4

I was daily trying to practice Philippians 4:6-7—that is not be anxious but ask God for what I needed with thanksgiving. In my quiet time and as I took my morning walk, I prayed about everything, named everything that I was thankful for, and asked him for what I needed. Truthfully, the peace came and went.

I began teaching ESL at my church two mornings a week for two hours. We had a good set of materials to use, and since I had taught for 20 years in Hong Kong, it was easy to prepare my lessons. I really enjoyed my contact with the students from different parts of the world. I could relate to them because I had spent time in class learning Chinese. Sometime after that, a fellow church member and I began a Sunday morning Bible class for internationals. For many Sundays, no one came. We continued to pray and to invite ESL students to come; finally, some began to come. I have continued with the class now for about 20 years. The students come and go, but we help them learn English and Biblical truths.

A short time later, when I attended the retreat for fellow retired missionaries, I had joyous reunions with many missionary friends and saw a large group of new missionaries appointed to serve in various countries.

I roomed with a former missionary colleague, Linda, and we had good times of sharing. During the conference, we were able to reconnect with many former colleagues and meet new people. Linda and I decided to stay over another day to have more time to talk and catch up. I shared with her about my upcoming surgery, and we prayed together. I knew she would continue to pray for me. That was a big comfort and encouragement. We parted ways to return to our respective homes but kept in contact.

Waiting was hard, but these experiences and people were a great help for me. God provided what I needed at every moment.

# DAY 38:

# A GLASS HALF-FULL

When my nephew saw my name with 'surgery' written by it on my sister's calendar, he was surprised. I had not told the family but had planned to tell them that weekend, a few days before the surgery, that I was having a lumpectomy.

As he was leaving that day, he asked me how old I was, and I told him 77. Then, he asked if I had ever been in the hospital, and I said no. Then he said to me, "Congratulations on being 77 and never having been in the hospital."

I thought to myself that this was a wonderful way to see it—the glass half-full. I went on to have successful surgery and have continued to be cancer-free.

Another time, I was chatting with a member of my Sunday School class. After she had complimented me on my dress, I thanked her, and as we talked further, I told her that most of my clothes were about 20 years old. She replied to me that she wished she could still wear clothes that she had 20 years ago. Again, I thought to myself that this was a wonderful way to look at it. I did have to work constantly to keep extra pounds off, but it was worth it. Wearing twenty-year-old clothes is not a bad price to pay for continuing to be active and healthy.

I have sometimes been accused of being a 'Pollyanna' because I tend to see the bright side in most situations. In fact, I have had a very blessed life with few great difficulties. However, sometimes, I wonder if that has been the case or if it is my attitude toward life that has made it seem so.

Paul said in Philippians 4:12-13: "I know what it is to be in need and I know what it is to have plenty. I have learned the secret of being content in any and every situation, whether living in plenty or in want. I can do everything through him who gives me strength." (NIV) Of course, the 'him' Paul is talking about is Jesus Christ.

May we all learn to put these words into effect as we live our lives day by day.

# ABOUT THE AUTHOR

Donna was born in Dekalb County, Georgia. When she was two years old, her father moved the family to a farm in Fayette County, Georgia.

The whole family became active in Fayetteville Baptist Church. She graduated from Fayette County High School, Truett McConnell Jr. College (now University), and Georgia State College (now University) with a BA in English and Secondary Education. She received her MRE from Southern Baptist Theological Seminary in May 1963.

She taught English and Speech at Otsego High School in Tontogony, Ohio, for 3 years and at the same time, she worked with a new church plant in Bowling Green, Ohio, that became Bowling Green Baptist Church.

In June 1966, she was appointed by the Foreign Mission Board of the Southern Baptist Convention (now the International Mission Board) as a missionary to Hong Kong, where she served for 36 years. After studying Cantonese (a Chinese dialect), she began teaching English and the Bible at a local Baptist high school and served in a local Baptist church. After a number of years, she and some members from that church helped develop a recently planted church, Chi Fu Baptist Church. Later, that church sent her and a group of members to plant and develop a church in a nearby large housing complex that became South Horizons Baptist Church. When that church had become stable, she joined a group from another church to work with some believers to help develop a recently planted church in a nearby very large government housing complex. She served there until her retirement in May 2002.

In 2009, she joined a Hong Kong Christian group to provide training for middle school English teachers in a city in southern China. In 2012, she retired again and is now living in a retirement community in Fayetteville, Georgia. She is an active member of Fayetteville First Baptist Church and teaches in their ESL ministry.

www.ingramcontent.com/pod-product-compliance
Lightning Source LLC
Chambersburg PA
CBHW051330120626
46547CB00016B/2474